I would if I cou

A humorous look at the funniest excuses people give.

By
JIM BRINKERHOFF

Illustrated by
ERIC BODEN

COMING
May 1997

"YOU KNOW YOU'RE A MORMON MOTHER IF..."

ISBN: 0-9653327-2-1

© 1997 Jim Brinkerhoff
Published by BF Publishing
391 Saint Simons Cove #202
Lawrenceville, GA 30244
1-800-270-2323

Acknowledgments

Many thanks to my family who have all taken an active interest in this publication. A very special thanks to my wife, Nancy, who has been more than supportive to me in the things I have wanted to do and in motivating me to finish this work on schedule. To Rebecca Arenas, who inspired me to write this book while making a passing comment in the halls of our church on a Sunday in October. To Kevin Goldsberry, for his countless hours working out the various enhanced computer programming stuff, of which I know little about. And, finally, to Bob Veals, whom I am proud to say is my brother-in-law, for his input and proofreading of this document.

A special thanks to those of you who are reading and enjoying this book for giving me a moment of your time to share some laughter and thoughts about some of the funny excuses we all use from time to time.

Table of Contents

Table of Contents

Introduction

♦ 1000 plus Mormon excuses

♦ 60 categories for immediate access

Have you ever asked someone to do something only to hear an excuse? You might even recognize some of the universal excuses I have put into this book--many are the actual excuses offered.

While we often think we have good reasons or excuses for not doing the things we know we should do, it is fun to stop for a moment and take a look at some of the funniest excuses used. People say the darndest things--particularly when they are not thinking or focused on what they are saying.

I would if I could, but...

The Bible teaches us that it is far better to say no and end up doing what we're supposed to, than to say yes and not do what is requested. Returning a simple telephone call to accepting a church calling are of the same priority when excuses are used to evade responsibility. Doing what you say you will do offers the highest degree of integrity possible.

This book has been written to look at the funny side of some of the many excuses people hear while directing, motivating and working with LDS people. Each of the sayings are best enjoyed if you will imagine them in the first person and say, "I would if I could, but..." before the saying.

I hope each of you will enjoy the following pages. Each drawing is the heading of a new alphabetized category. This 127-page book of over 1000 excuses is sure to cause you to think about what you will say the next time you are asked if you got your Home Teaching accomplished for the month—"I would if I could, but..." I've been reading this crazy book!

Jim Brinkerhoff 1997

<u>Accepting Callings</u>

I don't feel right about this.
are you sure you were inspired?
is this inspiration or desperation?
that would take too much of my time.
I am not prepared.
I have no tolerance for that.
no, thank you anyway.
I don't believe I can do what you expect me to do.
I have trouble understanding and comprehending.
people don't respect me.
I'll accept the call, but I won't do it.
I would **never** do that!
my health would not allow me to do it.
I'm a follower not a leader.
I just come to church—I don't want to work.
I have no ambition to lead the congregation.
teaching a class is out of the question.
my cat died and it will take some time to get over it.
my kids have their orthodontist appointments that night.
my husband does all the callings in this family.

I would if I could, but...

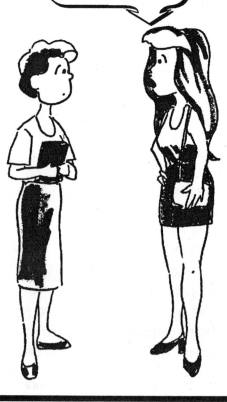

I would if I could, but...

Attending Church Colleges

it's too far away from home.
I don't have any winter clothes.
I couldn't get in anyway.
BYU only wants Jocks and Brains.
I wouldn't know what to do without my friends.
my brain is filled with High School stuff.
my dresses would not meet the code.
I would have to shave—but tattoos are okay if you play sports.
I want to meet some real people, that's why I like Utah State.
Rick's is out of the question—it's a junior college!
I don't want to take any more religion classes.
I need to go to a school that is accredited in my field of choice.
my parents went there.
I have got to have my car.
I don't agree with the dress code.
it's not where my friends are going.
Idaho is in country bumpkin.
I'm not a member.
my parents want me to go there, and I want to do other things.

<u>Baptism</u>

I can't remember the prayer.
I don't know how to hold them.
I feel like I am drowning them.
the clothes never fit, and I've got to look good.
people would see through my wet white clothes.
that's reserved for the missionaries.
I can't get rid of my sins, let alone baptize someone else.
I am not ready for a heavy duty commitment.
my hair would get wet.
I can't breathe under water.
other churches just sprinkle.
I'm not strong enough to hold them under.
there is never enough water.
I've already taken a bath.
I think that I am coming down with something.

Basketball

I don't have the time for practice.
church basketball is too rough.
I lose my religion when I play.
basketball courts should not be in churches.
I don't play on carpet floors.
I won't play without a coach.
I won't play with a coach.
the games and schedules are not organized.
religion and sports don't mix.
the last time I played, I lost this tooth.
I won't play with Brother...
that is a "hot head" sport, and I am trying to be Christlike.
you never have enough good players.
practice is always too late.
practice is always too early.
I used to wrestle instead.
church basketball impedes my eternal progression.
I don't need a license to kill.
it would be easier to sell me tickets on the next space shuttle.
church basketball builds tension and relieves frustration.
you would not want me on your team.
I can't handle the psychological pressure.

Bishopric Meetings

it's too early in the morning.
there is no agenda.
the Bishop just rambles on.
I spend too much time on other things.
my wife never wakes me up.
I keep forgetting.
they never follow the agenda.
I can't get ready in time.
I never can remember what Sunday it is.
I like to spend time with my family instead of in meetings.
those meetings never accomplish anything.
there is no need for me to be there.
they won't miss me anyway.
I have not missed a meeting in 19 years, cut me some slack!
it's just another meeting in my busy schedule.
we talk, make assignments, we talk, make assignments, etc. etc.
that is my only time to sleep in.
let the counselors relay the message to me.
I couldn't get my shoe laces untied.

I would if I could, but...

<u>Blessing the Sacrament</u>

I can't read the prayer.
the microphone makes me nervous.
my hands are dirty.
I thought the youth did that.
you need to ask one of the kids—they need the practice.
I pray with my eyes closed.
it really is hard for me to read the prayer.
I don't like to participate in such an important event.
I am really having a hard day.
have you asked the brother over there?
I have a sore throat.
I don't feel right about reading the prayers.
isn't there anyone else?
I haven't done that for 50 years and it is hard for me to see.
I don't know how small to break the bread.
I never learned the prayer.
the words make me stutter.
I got married last week and want to sit with my new wife.

Cannery Assignment

you need to ask the unemployed to do it.
my spouse has other plans.
the kids won't let us.
I don't believe the church should be in the Cannery business.
I have no idea where it is.
I am out of gas this month.
this is my only night at home.
I was thinking about starting back to school that day.
I can't commit because I don't know what I will be doing.
let the welfare people carry the load.
I really am not into cleaning up after canning chili.
I have someone in the Hospital I need to visit.
I was going Home Teaching then—which do you want?
I believe those in need should work that assignment.
I don't like the supervisor, so until that changes count me out.
the equipment is antiquated.
the church spends more time and energy than it's worth.
if we don't do it, they may get the idea and sell it.
I am going to be sick that night.
I don't have cannery-type work clothes.
my kids are all sick, and I need to be here to help them.

Chaperones

that is what the leaders are called to do.
I haven't the time to spend trying to regulate church standards.
you should ask the parents of those who are going.
that is my date night with my wife.
we just drop our kids off and go shopping those nights.
I really don't understand the youth.
I am too strict—no one would have fun.
I only listen to classical music.
have those who planned the activity do the chaperoning.
my kids need little chaperoning.
its not like it used to be.
I don't need more stress in my life.
my kids are not going tonight.
I wouldn't want to impose on the Elders Quorum.
I told the missionaries I would split with them.

I would if I could, but...
Sister Beals always sings to her own notes.

Choir

it takes time away from my family.
I can't sing.
I don't like to sing in front of people.
the director is not any good.
I don't like the songs they sing.
there is no challenge for me.
there are too many people anyway.
there are not enough people.
I can't leave children home alone.
I have too many other meetings.
practice is during my nap time.
we always have our family over at that time.
my kids are too small.
if I sang there would be no one left to sing to.
I can't carry a tune in a bucket.
I only like to sing on Sundays.
the baby-sitters can't handle my kids.
you're doing such a good job without me.
I do enough singing at church.
I always get laryngitis when I sing.
my talent is not singing, and I should give up trying to develop it.
I can't read music.
it is always too hot next to all those singers.
I don't want to try out or be called on to sing a solo.
my voice cracks when I sing.
I am happier when I listen to the others.

<u>Clean up Committee</u>

just let the janitors do it.
I was on the "getting there" committee.
I cleaned up last time.
that's what the Elders are supposed to do.
why does it need to be cleaned up?
I would just leave it for the other Wards to do.
the vacuum doesn't work.
let the ladies do it.
I won't come if I have to clean up.
I have got to get home for another appointment.
it's way past my kids' bedtime.
I wish you would have asked sooner.
the party was great and I have to catch an airplane.
my doctor said I should not do any exercise.
the young parents need to clean their kid's mess.
I thought the new program pays for it to be done.
I am late as it is now, thanks for asking.

<u>Conference</u>

I will read it in the Church Magazines.
it is too crowded.
I never get a seat.
I don't like sitting on hard chairs.
all the good seats are taken.
I can't hear in the back.
no changes are being made.
it is the same thing every conference.
I like to hear motivational speakers.
that is the only Sunday I have a chance to stay home and rest.
I stay home so others will have a seat.
the Stake center is too far away.
I know what they are talking about anyway.
conferences nowadays shouldn't require as much time.
we have only been commanded to attend Sacrament meeting.
my brother-in-law didn't pick me up.

Curfews

I ran out of gas.
the oil light came on and I didn't want to start the car.
I got lost.
I forgot it was daylight savings time.
my date wouldn't let me out of the car.
I lost track of the time.
there are no clocks at the church.
someone said I could be late.
my date's car lights would not work so we had to walk home.
the car wouldn't start—it was flooded or something.
we were just in the driveway.
my friend broke up with her boyfriend and I had to comfort her.
the traffic was really bad.
I missed the last bus.
I was trying to be early for Seminary.
I fell asleep on her couch.
I must have taken a wrong turn.
they said it was only 11 o'clock the last time I checked the time.
it was raining out, so I waited until it was over.
it lasted longer than I would have ever imagined.
you wouldn't want me to be rude and leave early.
he will think I am a geek if I tell him I have to be home.
I got the worst case of constipation and nearly went to the hospital.
we were trying to meet them but couldn't find them anywhere.
one of the wires on my braces came off and the time just slipped away.

<u>Dating</u>

I am only 14.
the girls are all geeks.
there are no cute boys in my Ward.
they said kissing at 16, not dating.
my parents have to go everywhere I go.
I'm married.
what kind of car do you have?
my parents wouldn't like the guy, anyway.
I have no money.
he has no money.
I wouldn't know what to wear.
I don't want my parents to meet her.
his pants sag so much they might fall off.
he looks like he lives in the 50's and talks like a valley girl.
but, but, major grease!
all the boys are taken.
none of the boys look at me.
she has been going with him since the beginning of time.
I don't have the car this weekend.
my dad backed over the road spikes and flattened the tires.
he never asked me.
I like you just as a friend.
I just washed my hair.
where did you go on your mission?
didn't we meet in the spirit world?
you're really nice, I just have to get my nails done.

Deseret Industries

their trucks drip oil all over my driveway.
I used to shop there.
every time I go over there I get depressed.
does Salt Lake think that all our stuff should be given to DI?
I like to buy new things.
all my things are worn out.
they wouldn't want my stuff.
I have 4 cars that don't run and DI won't take them.
all the good stuff is gone.
nothing fits me.
I give it to DI this week, then buy it back the next week.
what would people say if I wore used clothes?
it's not convenient.

<u>Dry Packing</u>

I don't like it.
it's too much trouble.
I am concerned about the sanitary conditions of my food.
I only eat prepared food.
I haven't the time.
I usually buy my food at the grocery store.
my children will not eat it.
I can't get off work.
I found that it is just as cheap to buy generic brands.
I only eat fat free foods.
my storage area is limited.
my diet is regulated by my doctor's orders.
we eat fresh healthy foods.
the food doesn't agree with my digestive system.
my doctor said I need to eat real food.

Emergency Preparedness

I am all ready for anything.
it will never happen to me.
I have a list at home, somewhere, I know.
tornadoes only hit mobile home parks.
I will get ready next week.
what will Salt Lake think of next?
I will have plenty of time after I see it on the weather channel.
I live on top of the hill.
I will as soon as my kids get accepted at BYU.
with all the problems I have lived through, what's another one?
why prepare now when tomorrow will bring much better news?
it's not the year 2000 and then it won't matter.
it's all in my attic.
I just think everything will be fine.
I am tired of preparing—this is the nineties.

<u>Fast Offerings</u>

I pay enough.
I don't like those little Deacons having to beg for money.
have them take some of my tithing for that department.
no one ever comes around to collect.
I thought that was a Mystery fund.
let them go to the Bishop's storehouse.
I thought you only paid that on Fast Meeting Sundays.
let Salt Lake fund the offerings.
I pay at the end of the year if I have extra.
I am short this month.
I have no change.
how much is it?—can't afford it, thanks anyway.
have them talk to the Bishop.
I don't get paid until the 15th of the month.
I'm leaving right now—can you come back?
I never eat breakfast so I don't have to pay.

Feeding Missionaries

when I went on my Mission, we fed ourselves.
we only have one car.
they live too far away.
I have to have dinner ready at 6 and they have appointments.
I can't go and get them.
the neighbors don't like them riding their bicycles on our street.
I can barely feed my family, let alone the missionaries.
they would not like my cooking.
I would have to clean my house.
my husband is always out of town.
my girls have too much interest in them.
we live on the top floor and the security won't allow them in.
let Salt Lake feed them, they're the ones who sent them here.
well..., the last time they were over...
I only raised girls—I can't afford 2 young men!
they just eat and run with no time to visit.

I would if I could, but...

Fireside

I have too much homework.
I don't like the speaker.
none of my friends are going.
I don't have anything to wear.
the boys act up too much.
it's boring.
we always hear what they are talking about.
I don't have fun.
the refreshments are gross.
I don't have transportation.
it's our Family Home Evening night.
my parents like me to stay home.
I always end up sitting on the floor and it hurts my back.
I've got a date, I think.
I am on a diet so I can't have refreshments.
my family is not going.

Food Storage

I have had it over the years, and it is all spoiled now.
I never eat it anyway.
we live in an apartment; my only storage place is under the bed.
I've got my water in my swimming pool.
my kids don't like pinto beans.
my freezer is full of stuff.
it just gets in our way.
I can't afford it.
I don't think it is worth the effort.
frankly, I am tired of the Church preaching gloom and doom.
you want food storage—look at my garage.
nothing will happen—this is modern days.
my son owns a grocery store.
I have no room to store things as it is now.
under my bed is a bit radical, don't you think?
I would rather devote that energy to raising my children.
I don't like wheat.
my kids won't eat it

I would if I could, but...

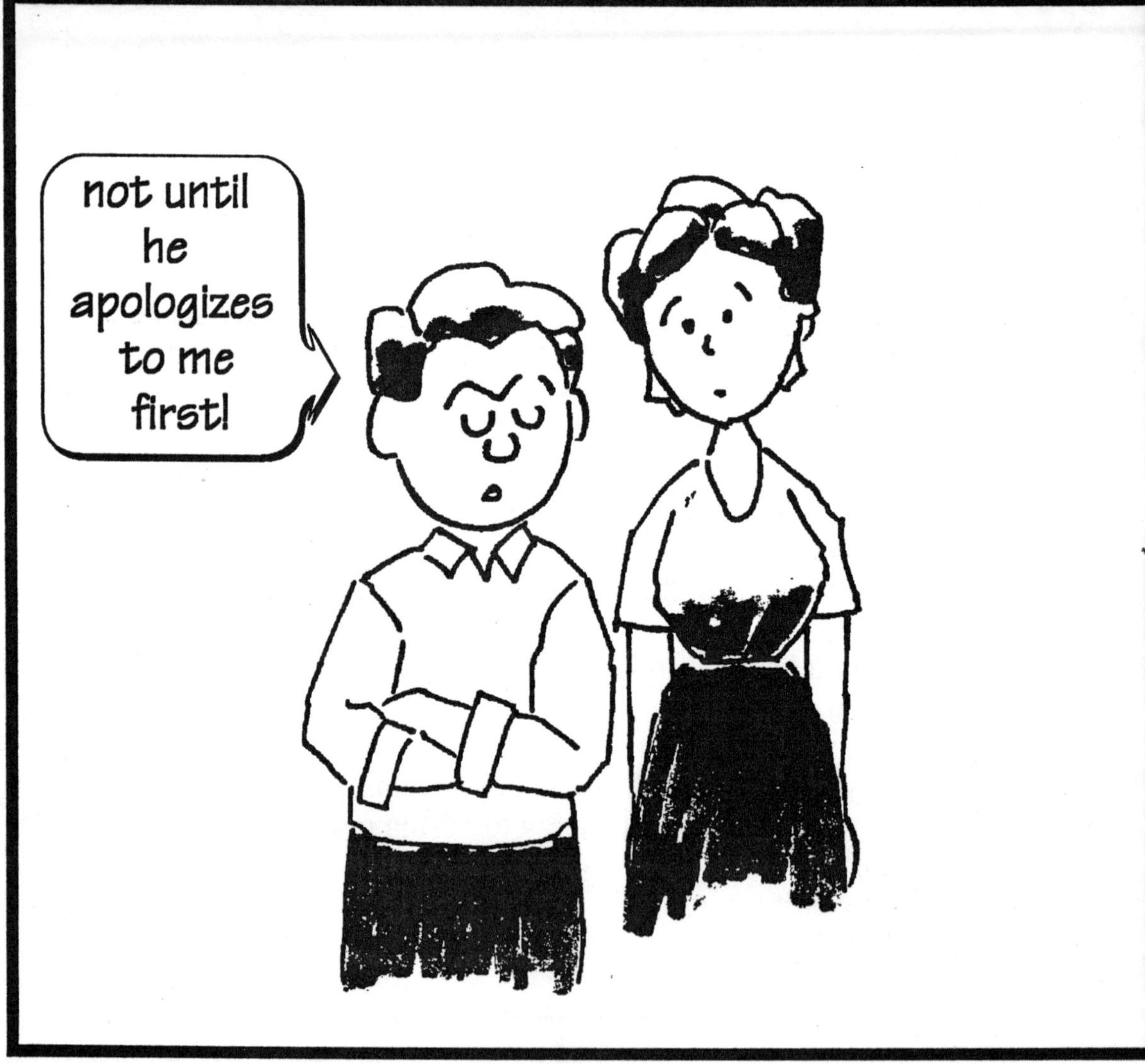

__Forgiving__

this goes back two generations.
after what he said about me?
I have exhausted all levels of tolerance.
he just won't talk to me.
she hasn't said she was sorry yet.
I can't bring myself around to it.
few people would do that after what has happened to me.
it's not in my heart.
communication is a one-way street with them.
I promised I would on my death bed.
I haven't got the time to work it out.
it doesn't bother me half as much as it does him.
he will have to apologize first.
I will after he pays me back the money he cost me.
she just talks bad about everyone.

I would if I could, but...

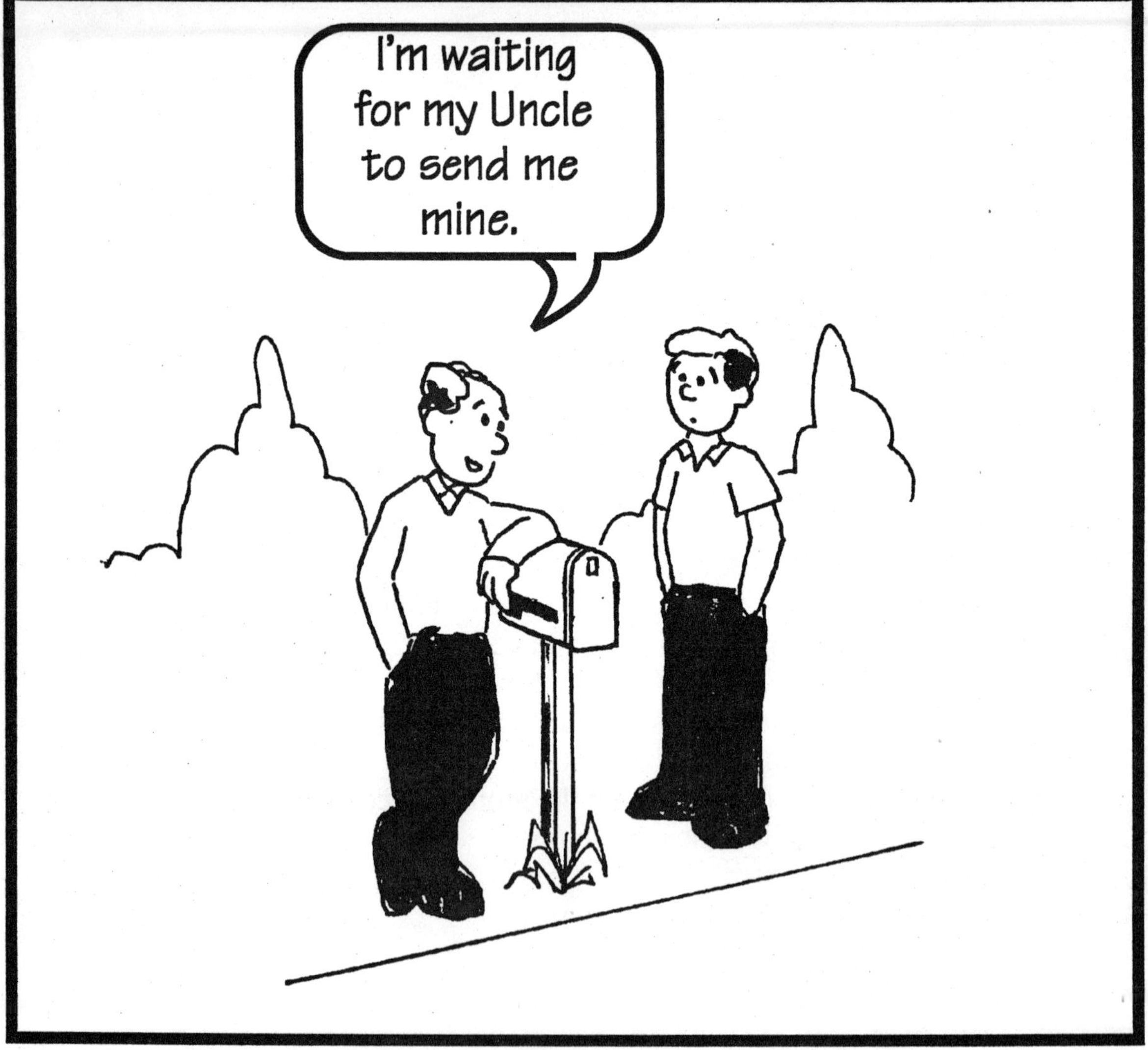

Genealogy

I have an Uncle that does mine for me.
I never could figure out the forms.
I don't have time to look people up.
I can't work a computer.
my eyes can't see the microfiche.
our family has no records.
I am the start of our family.
my kids can do that.
I have no interest in dead relatives.
I am too busy raising my kids.
my spouse likes me to spend the time at home.
most of our relatives are dead anyway.
our work has been done.
I don't have a copier and the church copier is broken.
I went canvassing once and got a wasp bite.
I am the only Mormon in my family.
He knows every hair on my head, surely He can figure it out.
I wouldn't want to offend someone who has passed away.
none of my relatives are important.

<u>Going on a Mission</u>

I would have to leave my girl friend.
I never learned how to ride a bike.
I would have to quit my job.
that is for the active men.
I have a life ahead of me.
I can't leave school right now.
I will after I get out of the Army.
my girlfriend just wouldn't understand.
I don't have any money.
I wouldn't know what to pack if I got sent down south.
I never was good at other languages.
I have a car payment.
I am still paying off my bills.
my apartment lease is for 3 years.
I would lose my identity if I got my hair cut.
I don't relate well with others.

<u>Going to Church</u>

I overslept.
I was out too late last night.
my insurance canceled, and I forgot to pay the premium.
my migraine headaches started up again.
it's too early.
it's too late.
it's SuperBowl Sunday.
the Braves are playing.
I forgot to turn my furnace on, and it was too cold.
it is always too hot in the Chapel.
there are too many kids.
people don't like me.
I have no calling.
the Bishop doesn't know me.
I have 500 other things to do.
the noise level is more than I can stand.
I have heard every dry councilman's talk since the beginning of time.
it was Ward Conference anyway.
I didn't feel well.
my car was broken down.
it's hunting season.
I was out of gas, and I have been taught not to buy on Sunday.
no one knows me.
I feel stupid sitting by myself.
the microphone hurts my hearing aid.
they need to have their meeting at a different time.
Sunday is the day I wash my car.
no one cares about me.
they never ask me to talk.
it annoys me not to start on time.
company came in and _they_ didn't have church clothes.

<u>Help Moving</u>

have the professionals do it.
my back hurts.
Saturday is my only day at home.
I don't want to take blessings away from the Elders Quorum.
I have to go downtown with my wife.
my kids have ball games.
they are never ready anyway.
maybe next time—I'm really busy.
my doctor said I should stay home.
if they are moving in, I only help people move out.
if they are moving out, I only help people move in.
why do you always ask me? Are the High Priests too old?
I helped last time and broke my toe.
my truck is in the shop, and it won't be back for several weeks.
I go hunting on Saturdays.
they are never prepared and it wastes my time.
someone in the neighborhood punctured two of my tires.

<u>Home Evening</u>

it's Monday night football.
I travel all week.
they don't send out new lesson manuals from Salt Lake.
it's just my wife and I.
there is never any time for me to prepare the lesson.
the kids just watch TV.
my family can't even get together to eat, much less for H.E.
I have homework that must get done.
I promised that I would go to the DQ with Suzy.
I can't get off the telephone long enough.
my social life would fall apart.
that's one more night I couldn't be with Cameron.
my dad just sleeps through the lesson anyway.
my family is too big—we have three kids, you know.
all the good TV programs are on that night.
that's the only night I have to be out with my friends.
I am in college now.

I would if I could, but...

Homemaking

my husband won't let me leave the house after dark.

I have to stay home and do my kids' homework.

I've been there and done that!

the kids really bother me when I go.

some of the ladies just go to gossip.

it's not Christmas time.

I have enough homemaking things to do around here.

the kids have the car that night.

my husband is working late.

little Johnny cries when I leave the house without him.

it's not in my budget this month.

it scares me to be out after dark.

I can only drive in daylight.

my grandkids always come over that evening.

my husband thinks I am needed at home so he can go play church basketball.

that is the time I clean my house.

sometimes a person has just got to say no to extra meetings.

they never do what I want to do.

I have done it all and now it is time to let the younger people do it.

my bones won't move like they used to.

I don't like to be a part of the cliquish groups.

my salvation does not require me to attend homemaking meeting.

my husband started to rebuild the engine in our car.

I would if I could, but...

Home Teaching

I forgot that it was the end of the month.
I lost my keys.
I have too many inactive families.
I never can get with my junior companion.
my companion is my wife, and she does not want to go.
I had a wedding and two funerals last month.
my families are never at home.
I can't get along with my families.
I have no common interest with the families I teach.
I feel like a burden to my families.
another night, another meeting, when will it all stop?
I am the worst procrastinator.
I promise I will get it done next month.
you keep changing my families so I never know who to visit.
I am now a High Priest.
they never give us the Ward Teaching messages anymore.
there is nothing I can do for my families.
I don't want my families to call for help—I'm too busy now.
they need to give me families that are in my circle of friends.
the end of the month just comes around too fast.
I would rather have quality than percentages.
I was out of town all month.
I spent all my Home Teaching time surfing the Internet.

I would if I could, but. . .

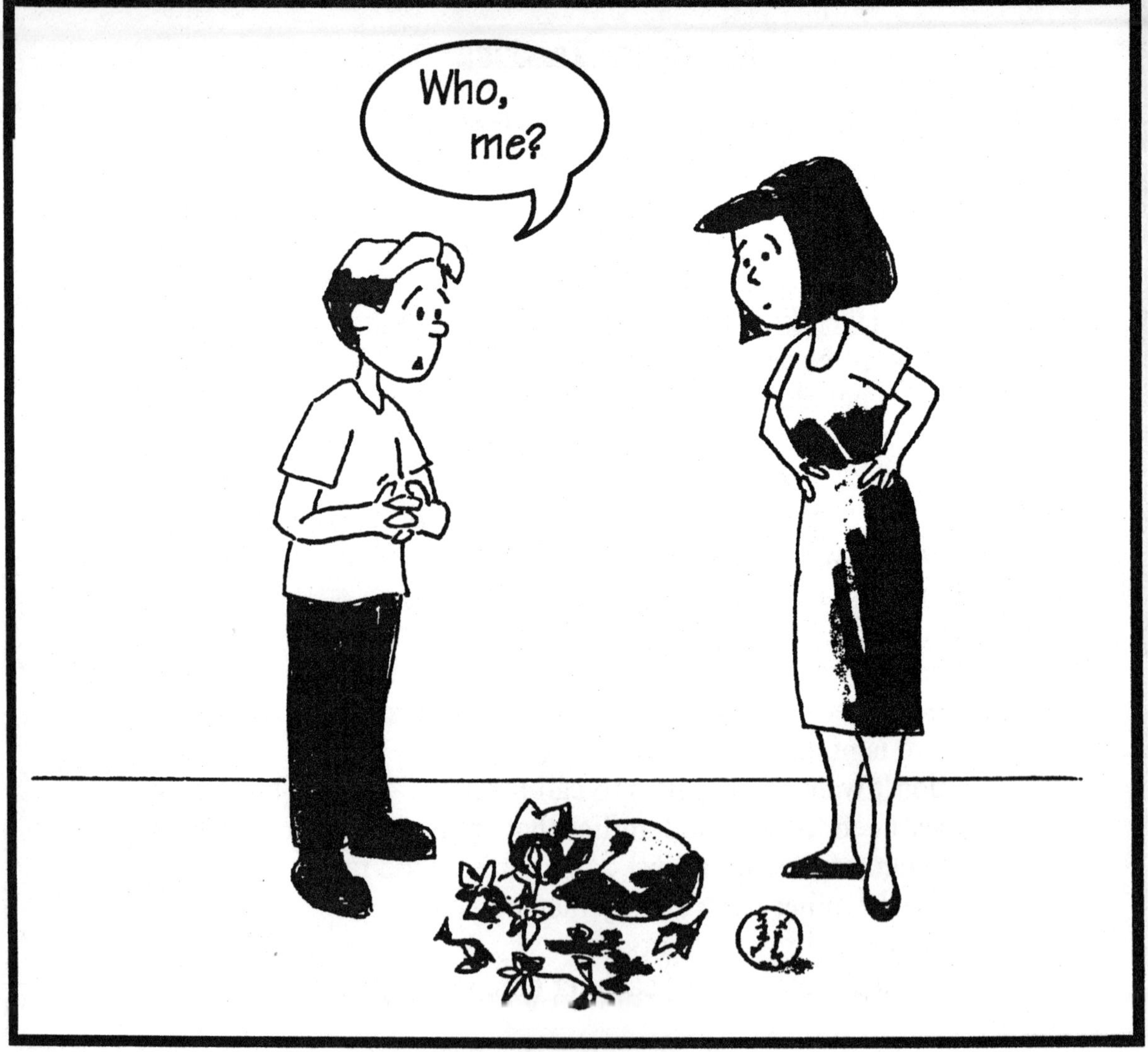

<u>Honesty</u>

would you define that?
I am honest, for the most part.
it's hard when everyone else does it.
they don't pay me enough anyway.
I am in this groove and I don't want to make any waves.
I have been taught to tell the truth even when it's wrong.
it's pretty much something I leave alone and let life take its
        course.
the devil himself made me do it.
you mean, ***totally*** honest?
my expense account is never checked.
I didn't do it, no one saw me do it.
it wasn't me!
my company allows me to take all the time off I need.
the office has it for our use.
I do all the copying at my office.

Library

I never find the time to go to the library now.
I have been instructed to only open the library for 10 minutes.
I will get it back as soon as I am done.
didn't little Johnny bring that back last week?
I don't remember taking that.
are you sure it was me?
I have never been back there.
I never can remember to bring those pencils.
I was having a bad hair day.
I took it home with me, and the dog ate it.
I didn't think I was supposed to return it.
I thought the copier was for everyone's use.
can you help me set up the church satellite to ESPN?
the pictures didn't go with the lesson.
I didn't have time to prepare a lesson--what video do you have?
I took the VCR home to watch football highlights and it broke.
why is all the chalk broken and in small pieces?
whatever happened to the Wollensack?
where is the Library, anyway?

I would if I could, but...

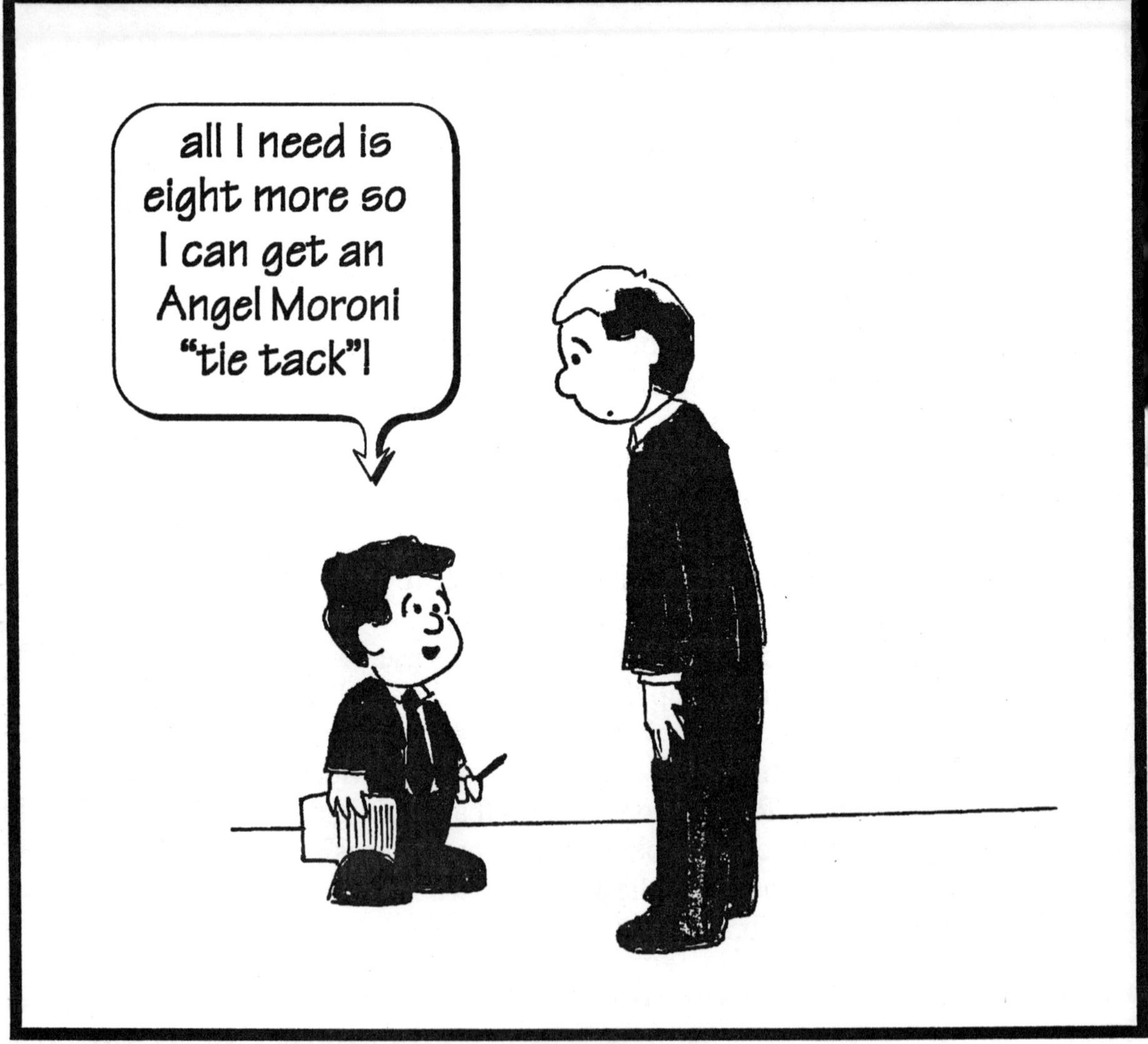

Magazines

Salt Lake has messed my account up so bad with the new
        billing system that I am just going to wait.
I never get a chance to read what I have now.
my expenses are out of control.
I have got to stop somewhere.
I think they are making too much money on them now.
I have to stretch my dollars to meet my needs.
church magazines are a low priority.
unless it is on TV, I don't read it.
I don't like getting hassled at church to buy magazines.
my kids are all grown.
there is no need, my son is the Bishop.
I don't have time to read my industry magazines.
I read my scriptures in the mornings and watch TV at night.
I don't like their dunning notices.
I like them mailed to me separately.
I just pick them up at Deseret Book when I need them.
I think the Reps must be on commission.
I don't like them selling stuff at church.
when will they be out on CD-Rom?

<u>Meetings</u>

there are too many meetings now.
I have responsibilities at home.
all the meetings are the same.
we end up talking about the same problems.
I didn't volunteer for this job and, particularly, not for more
      meetings.
they were better with the other Bishop.
we seem to just call meetings to have more meetings.
going to more meetings will not fit into my schedule.
the more meetings I go to the further I get behind.
meetings are a Mormon's way of life, and I need to slow down.
it's a bigger time waster than my computer.
if I had this many meetings in my business, nothing would get done.
we meet to greet and greet to meet.
I never have anything to say.
I don't want to say anything that may disrupt the spirit.
meetings tend to drag on, and on, and on, and on.
I get annoyed with people who bring up stupid stuff.
what is important to some is not important to me.
no one told me about the meeting.
I don't have a ride home.

I would if I could, but...

Missionary Splits

I served my mission.
it takes too much of my time.
I didn't go on a mission, because I don't like tracting.
I only have a convertible.
my car has got so much stuff in it, only I can fit.
I thought they had a car.
I have no interest in preaching.
my reputation in the community will not allow me to go.
I have no common interest.
all we do is ride around and visit members.
I don't know the discussions.
I don't like praying in front of strangers.
people may think I am weird hanging around the missionaries.
we never did that when I was on my mission.
my wife has the car that night.
my car insurance doesn't cover the missionaries.
I have done my Home Teaching for the month.
it looks like another something to keep me from staying home.
I only wear a tie on Sundays.
it's too late when I get home from work.
I'm never home.
I have other plans scheduled.
the mission rules state that they need to be together.

Nursery

I have raised my kids—I do not need another experience.
my doctor said I need to have less stress in my life.
I come to church to worship, not baby-sit.
let the parents tend their own kids.
the room is too small and the toys are all broken.
I raised one child and I don't need to do it again.
I really hate changing dirty diapers.
why are you doing this to me?
I would rather eat concrete than to watch her kids.
I would not know what to cook for dinner.
I don't like kids.
I've served my time, thank you.
changing dirty diapers is not my bag!
that calling is for the newly weds who have yet to experience
       crying babies, dirty diapers, and out of control kids.
their baby is so spoiled.
they never play together like older kids.
I thought they did away with a nursery.

PPI Meeting

I don't do Peter Priesthood Interviews (PPI).
I don't need to find out what I am not doing.
it interferes with my Sunday School class.
I am too nervous when they talk to me.
I don't like telling someone my faults.
I don't need anything from them.
just call me at home.
my report is not as good as it could be—it **will** be better next
    month.
my Home Teacher asks the same questions.
a yearly Temple interview is enough for this lifetime.
I don't have time, because I need to be sure my kids are in
    class.
I promised I would take my son to McDonald's.
my back has been hurting all week, so I need to sit on soft
    chairs.
my life is too personal.
I just want to know who came up with the idea of "interviews"!
interviews and meetings—a Mormon way of life!

<u>Passing the Sacrament</u>

I am not dressed appropriately.
that is for the Deacons to do.
I don't know the system.
I would be too nervous.
I don't like watching other people eat.
that is my time to meditate.
I don't want to.
it would interfere with my nap.
I got up too late.
my hair isn't combed.
I wore my cowboy boots today.
I don't have a tie.
I didn't shave today.
I don't have a white shirt.
in the past I have never got it right.
my doctor said I need to avoid pressures.

<u>Prayer</u>

I wouldn't know what to say.
I don't do well in front of people.
I only pray privately.
prayers are personal.
I won't be here on time.
my kids won't let me.
I have got to save our bench for my family.
my prayers don't even reach to the ceiling.
I only know the Lord's prayer.
I never seem to get an answer, so I've given up.
it hurts my knees.
I have to play the organ.
I really get nervous in front of all the people.
I am not in the mood today.
my spirituality is low—that's why I'm here.
I have a cold.
I said it last week.
I can never get our family together.
my husband is not very supportive.
it's really hard to get everyone settled down.

I would if I could, but...

Priesthood Committee Meetings

I don't know what committee I am on.
none of the committees interest me.
we never get anything accomplished.
it seems like another time to waste more time.
I only like to meet with the Elders.
I am not comfortable around the High Priests.
I like the regular Priesthood lessons.
the Bishop never goes, so why should I?
that is the time I can visit with my friends.
the Stake people usually dominate the meetings.
if the teacher gets a break on that Sunday, I should also get one.
that gives me a chance to be with my children without missing
        Priesthood meeting.
that is the only time I can visit with the *other* Ward's members.
nothing ever gets done.
I have my own committee meeting.
that is the time I use for PPIs.
I usually run home to check on dinner.

I would if I could, but...

"R" Rated Movies

PG-13 is much worse.
there is no action in the other movies.
I like the excitement.
all the good movies are rated "R".
there is more sex and skin in PG-13s than in "R".
it's my choice and I think they are fine.
my parents won't let me.
I'm not 17 yet.
they are talking about the late night "R" rated movies on TV.
my friends are all going.
it's just someone's interpretation.
my whole life is "R" rated.
I just close my eyes at the bad parts.
there is NOTHING else playing and it's our first date.
it doesn't apply with the new TV rating system.
that was an old rule when the "R" rating was bad.
"R" means restricted for maturity—not for the kids.
I am sure they meant "X" rated.

I would if I could, but...

<u>Read the Lesson</u>

no one does.
the teacher never follows the lesson anyway.
there are too many interruptions in the meaning of the lesson.
it confuses me, because I cannot follow the teacher.
I never know what lesson to read.
I lost my lesson book.
I keep my scriptures and my lesson manuals in my briefcase
      so I won't forget them.
I like to hear what the teacher thinks about the lesson.
why should I, the teacher will read it to us.
the teacher never lets me talk about what I want to talk about.
it's the same lesson year after year.
no one can beat the recycling job the church does with manuals.
I loaned it to my wife.
I always have trouble reading aloud.
I didn't bring my reading glasses.
my glasses broke and I haven't got my new ones yet.
I don't even have five minutes to read my scriptures.
the dog ate the lesson manual.
I had the same lesson last week at another Ward.

<u>Relief Society</u>

I have to go home and cook dinner.
that is the time I use to clean up after Sunday School.
I leave after Sunday School.
the room is too crowded.
I don't agree with Sister...
she always tells us about her kids and how great they are.
I can never sit by my friends.
the chairs are too close together.
I don't enjoy listening to Molly Mormons.
self-righteousness is not going to be a part of my life.
I can do without the fellowship.
I liked it better when we met separately and the working
       mothers weren't there.
there are too many personalities involved.
I don't want to interrupt because I can never get there on time.
you know I have a lot of children that depend on me.
there is no one my age in there.
that is for the older women.
the room is always cold.
the room is always hot

I would if I could, but...

Road Show

there is no talent in our Ward.
it would require way too much time.
the kids don't want to do it.
I thought they quit doing Road Shows years ago.
I would do it first class, and the budget wouldn't allow it.
the kids like to play basketball instead.
no one wants to do the parts.
it's just not fun.
I can't write the script and direct the show, too.
my patience level would not handle it.
I like the youth without the involvement.
it's too much trouble.
you should have asked me two months ago.
our new chapel doesn't have a stage.
the kids want perfection without practice.
our Bishop is the only comedian in our Ward.
the party afterwards is the best part.
my doctor said I should not involve myself with hectic things.

<u>Scouting</u>

my sons are involved in school sports.
my kids are spoiled—they like to sleep in Holiday Inns.
the scout leader never shows up on time.
the meetings are not organized.
there is nothing there for my kids.
I never liked scouts, either.
it is too hard to keep up with my school work.
no college scholarships are awarded for being a scout.
it starts late and ends early.
scouting is mass confusion in my eyes.
they seem to think that all of us like sleeping on the ground.
my boys like the activities with the girls.
if scouting is so good, why don't the girls do it?
it's too regimented.
the scoutmaster always borrows my pickup anyway.
isn't that an attitude thing?
there are too many non members running it.
there are two types of people—the doers and the don'ters.
I don't like boys.
I'm already too far behind—I could never catch up.
it's always on the wrong night.

Scripture Study

I don't have a triple combo.
the print is too small.
I have already read them once years ago.
it's hard to hold my attention, especially in Isaiah.
I gave my scriptures to my kids to use.
my glasses are never in the right place.
I need new glasses.
I will when I get to bed earlier.
the reading is not easy.
I never have the time to sit and contemplate.
they haven't come alive for me.
I am still trying to read the Bible.
I can never finish them.
my distractions are overwhelming.
I'm not a reader.
must we be commanded in all things?
I read every Sunday afternoon between the games.
I have had enough reading for this lifetime.
I am waiting for the video.

Seminary

it's too early.
I do my homework in the mornings.
I work late and need my sleep.
I can't stay awake.
I don't have a ride to school.
my mother won't get up to get me there.
I get my church on Sunday.
I take other classes instead.
I need my sleep to be sharp for school.
it is just another Sunday School class.
I will get it when I go to college.
there was no gas in the car.
the electricity went off in the night and the alarm didn't go off.
my kids are old enough to make their own decision.
if they want to go bad enough, they'll get themselves up.
my mother didn't hear my alarm clock.
it didn't get scheduled at school.
my doctor said for a clear complexion I need my sleep.
it's too cold in the mornings.
it's my blanket—I have to wrestle with it to let me out of bed.

<u>Seventy-Two Hour Preparation</u>

I have had it with food storage.
I can survive fine for seventy-two hours.
I don't need more stuff in my basement.
nothing will happen that I can't handle.
all they have to do in SLC is think up more things for us to do.
someone is making big bucks off this.
it won't do any good—my family would rather starve.
I will just get a hotel room.
I will just call my Home Teacher.
what is the Bishop's storehouse for?
I have gas in the car and water in the swimming pool.
my grocery is open 24 hours a day.
I've got all this stuff and don't know how to cook it.
I can't keep batteries in the GameBoy much less a flashlight.
our local radio station goes off the air at 6:00 pm.
extra blankets—I'll just take them off the beds.
hasn't SLC heard about ATM's?
my therapist said not to worry about it.

I would if I could, but...

Social Services

just because I have been out of work doesn't mean I need to go.
they never have any good jobs there.
our marriage is beyond Social Services' help.
it's too far.
what possible help can they give me.
their programs never seem to work.
if I go they end up scheduling me to work at the cannery.
I don't need help.
I can do it myself without someone telling me their opinions.
I've always wondered how they got those jobs, anyway.
we really are on a tight schedule with all the kids, you know.
no one seems to be able to give us help with our son.
we are too busy to take time off work.
I am already seeing a therapist.
my car battery is dead so I couldn't possibility get over there.
my spouse won't go.
we were too busy painting the house.
I had a hair appointment.
if I went, people would talk about me.
I really don't expect them to help me pay my bills.
do you think I am crazy, or something?

<u>Softball</u>

there is no place to practice.
the games are never on time.
I never enjoyed sports.
that is for the younger men in the Ward.
I know nothing about playing softball.
the umpires are authoritarians.
it lacks a bit of organization.
I don't want to go and sit on the bench and when you see me
        play that is where I would be.
the games interfere with my rest time.
the last time I played softball I broke my leg.
my game is golf.
the uniform wouldn't fit.
my kids would laugh at me.
I will watch instead.
my doctor said any exercise should be done slowly at my age.
is the "hot head" from 14th Ward playing?

<u>Speak at Sacrament Meeting</u>

I would rather die.
I have nothing to say.
I don't know anything about the topic.
my time won't allow me to prepare properly.
public speaking is not my forte.
no one wants to hear me.
I made a deal the last time I spoke that no one would ask me
    again.
I was planning to be out of town that weekend.
we were going to the lodge that Sunday.
I don't have anything prepared and there is no time.
three weeks is not enough time to allow me to get organized.
I spoke last Fast and Testimony meeting.
I have a Stake calling now.
they don't want me to talk about my trip I took last summer.
I don't speak English.
I want to preach from the Bible saying Amen Brother!

Stacking Chairs

I believe no physical activity should be done on Sunday.
I paid the budget to have the janitors do it.
just leave them down for the other Ward.
my doctor said I cannot lift anything.
let the janitor vacuum around them.
I never work in my Sunday clothes.
I am trying to keep the Sabbath day holy.
are the janitors on strike?
each time the chairs are stacked it shortens the life of the chairs.
the Elders Quorum does a good job doing that.
I liked it better with just our Ward meeting here.
I hurt my wrist playing Ward basketball.
it really boils down to the fact that, I just don't want to!
I don't mind folding chairs, I don't like to stack them.
that is not keeping the Sabbath Holy, in my opinion.
SLC needs to pay the janitors more money to stack chairs.
let the basketball players do it.
I'm short on comprehending the difference between stacking
        chairs and working in my yard on Sundays.
isn't the PFR guy supposed do all that?

I would if I could, but...

Sunday School

it's during the time I have to visit friends.
I have got to be at another Ward house.
I am in the Stake, now.
there is no teacher.
we only sit around and play hangman.
the kids don't go to my school.
even though the teacher is nice, she can't hold my attention.
I can't hear.
the teacher mumbles.
I get more out of it if I stay home and read the scriptures.
that's our time to go to the 7-11.
I need to monitor the halls.
I hold my own in the foyer.
I am making sure all the kids are in their classes.
someone has got to watch the front door.
I have to go home and prepare lunch for my family.
the teacher is boring.
the teacher doesn't bring treats.
the age groups don't correspond with the school's years.

<u>Temple Night</u>

I don't have a recommend.
I work in the evenings.
I have done the work for my family.
those nights are the nights I have set aside for my activities.
I don't have any clothes.
I would rather go to the movies.
it's too long a drive.
I have given up too many evenings as it is now.
I will do it when I have some names.
I can't leave the children alone for that long.
I let the High Priests do that.
I will go again when they change the movie.
I just loved the devil in the first movie.
I haven't done my genealogy.
I am not qualified.
I don't have the deal memorized.
I end up sleeping.
it's hard for me to understand all the commitments.
I'm also a Mason.

Tithing

I can't.
I pay in other types of services.
my budget is jammed with bills that have to be paid.
Salt Lake doesn't need the money.
have them take it out of the million dollar BYU scoreboard.
I don't support the church education program.
it should be voluntary, not mandatory.
I would rather give to the poor myself.
ten percent is too much money.
I just bought a new car.
my kids need braces.
I am always one paycheck behind.
I pay every year on my increase—I've just had no increase.
do you know the cost of raising kids nowadays?
I don't like where SLC spends the money.
my money needs to go to help the needy, not the dead.
my checkbook is at the office.
all my bills are paid by my accountant and he is not Mormon.
I wasn't taught to give like that.
I never agreed with McKay or Kimball or whoever it was on
        making it mandatory.

<u>Tithing Settlement</u>

I am sure the church records are correct.
I don't need to pay anymore.
there is nothing to settle.
the time is not convenient.
when is the church going to settle up with me?
we can't make another trip to the Ward house.
have them go on without me.
I don't need the exposure with the Bishop.
I don't want to take up his time.
I will go when they make it voluntary.
it seems like they always want more money, so I stay home.
my family is in from school during the holidays.
I will be out of town that whole time.
none of my questions ever get answered anyway.
they're too busy to see me.
I might miss some of the Christmas Specials on T.V.
that's just for the super active members.
I'm waiting for SLC to disclose *their* records to me.

<u>Usher</u>

people like to sit where they want to.
I enjoy the time to myself before Sacrament meeting.
let the Elders do that.
that would be a good job for the missionaries.
I am having trouble with my knee.
I have a new pair of shoes on and they hurt my feet.
ushers seem to have no effect on the noise level.
we have been instructed to sit with our families so that is what I
      am going to do.
I would have to shake hands and I smashed my thumb
      yesterday.
there are never enough seats anyway.
too many people save their own seats.
I'm really not very sociable.
it seems like the little Deacons could do that.
the entrance and exits are not positioned correctly.
I am not the missionary type.
I might catch cold, in and out and all.

<u>Visiting Teaching</u>

I can't go into the house because of my allergies.
my husband won't let me go.
my families won't let me in.
I can't go with all the children.
I don't have a driver's license.
I work.
I work two jobs.
I work three jobs.
I feel like I have to take a gift.
they have cats and I get sick.
my husband drives the car.
she talks too fast and I can never get a word in edgewise.
it kills a full day just visiting with Sister...
I don't know where they live.
my companion always shops that day.
I have to be near a telephone in case my husband calls.
my doctor said I shouldn't be around other people.
I would have to clean up my house if they come.

<u>Ward Correlation Meeting</u>

it is during the time I have to fix lunch.
Sundays after church is our family day.
we never get anything resolved.
the church is automatic and will run without me.
the Primary President always dominates the time.
the Bishop is always late.
this meeting is one that could and should be eliminated.
it's another excuse for failure.
I'm having trouble correlating with my family, right now.
it's a good idea that never gets action.
I could say what they say in half the time.
seems to me that all that gets done is correlating.
another meeting where we say we do or will, then don't.
I have had my allotment of meetings this month.
just have the missionaries do it—they have the time.

I would if I could, but...

Ward Party

I don't know anyone.
there are too many little kids running all over.
there is never a program.
I don't like group games.
I forgot what time it was.
I am tired of eating green Jell-O.
I am too tired.
they won't miss me anyway.
it never starts on time.
I might have to clean up afterwards.
I just can't get out of the house.
I don't need the fellowship.
I don't like the people who go to parties.
it would cause me to visit with people I don't know.
I only go to parties at Christmas.
it's too crowded.
there are never enough tables or chairs.

I would if I could, but...

Word of Wisdom

it's just words of wisdom for my discretion.
I don't think that cup of coffee will keep me out of heaven.
no one said we had to be perfect.
I don't know what Emma was thinking of—I **can** hit the
      spittoon.
my only addiction consists of diet caffeine-free Pepsi.
chocolate is worse than my coffee.
the Indians smoked.
my doctor said a small glass of wine at dinner was good for me.
I only drink the hard stuff when I have a cold.
I only do it for medicinal purposes which is okay.
I have tried everything and just can't do it.
it's cold in the mornings and Postem doesn't quite cut it.
my doctor said I have a chemical imbalance, so I need my tea.
but it's decaffeinated!
bringing in the new year wouldn't be the same without just a
      sip of wine.
I promise I will only drink Champagne at my kid's weddings.
did someone see me?

<u>Work at the Church Farm</u>

I think they should let the farmers do the work.
there are a lot of people who need jobs—let them do it.
that is my only day to play golf.
I am more of an inside-type person.
let Salt Lake get laborers to do it.
I never liked apples.
working outside makes me break out with sores.
my insurance wouldn't let me drive a tractor.
I have my own farm to work.
I always get poison ivy when I go and work.
I don't like snakes or alligators and they don't like me.
they planted the trees too far apart.
it's a bad year—they should just plow it under.
done that, been there!